Naughty Childr

Teacher's Book

by Janet Warburton
Pupil's Book by Alison Hawes

Contents

PEARSON
Longman
Edinburgh Gate
Harlow, Essex

No! said Mo

Guided Reading (session 1)

Key Objective

- Describe story settings and incidents and relate them to their own experience and that of others.

Each child will need Copymaster 1.
The teacher will need an enlarged copy of Copymaster 1.

Introduction

- Ask children to look at the front cover of the book and read the title together. Discuss the meaning of 'naughty'. *What have you ever done that you think is naughty? Is it the same as 'bad' or 'wicked'?*
- Ask children to look quickly through the whole book. *Where do these stories happen? Are they real places or made-up ones, like fairy stories? What kind of characters do they have in them?* [For example, real people rather than talking animals.]
- Explain that we are going to read the story called 'No! said Mo'. *Where is this story set? What can you see? Does it look like your school? What is the same/different about it?*
- **Strategy Check**: Recap the range of contextual and phonic strategies the children know. Identify the word 'Bun' on page 2 and ask the children to count and say the phonemes. Point out 'fun' and discuss how knowing one word can help us read another. Remind them to use the pictures and what they know about their own school to help work out difficult words.

Reading and Discussion

- Ask children to turn to pages 2 and 3. Lead children in reading the text together. *How does Mo feel? How do you know?*
- Ask them to read pages 4 and 5 alone. Praise successful reading of the pages and point out the new word 'music'.
- Ask children to read pages 6 to 9 alone, and then to show their partners the changed/new words on each page.
- Read pages 10 and 11 together, noticing a change now in the pattern.

Returning to the Text for Evaluation and Analysis

- Praise children for specific success in using different strategies.
- Ask children to think about why Mo is called 'naughty'. Using the enlarged Copymaster 1, select key events from the story and consider what they show about how Mo is feeling. Model for children choosing an incident and very briefly drawing or describing it. Discuss why they think Mo behaved like this, e.g. she was scared, lonely, worried, etc.
- Explain that you would like them to keep thinking about what Mo did through the school day and how she felt at the time. [Place some sticky notes asking about Mo, at intervals, on the classroom door, etc.].

No! said Mo

Guided Reading (session 2)

Key Objectives

- Describe story settings and incidents and relate them to their own experience and that of others.
- Recognise the critical features of words, including common spelling patterns.

Each child will need Copymaster 1 from session 1.

Introduction

- Remind children of the story read in the previous session. *How does Mo feel about going to school? Does she feel differently at the end of the story?*
- Ask children what was special about the way the story was written which helped them to read it [patterns of words with very few of them changed]. *Find an example and show it to your partner.*
- Look at pages 2 and 3 together and ask children what else helps them to read the words. [The rhymes.]
- Remind children that in the previous session we agreed that a rhyme could help us read more words. *If you can read 'Bun' then you can read 'fun'.* Focus their attention on the 'un' pattern.
- **Strategy Check**: Recap the range of contextual and phonic strategies the children know. Introduce and demonstrate your own word wheel and ask children to read other words ending in 'un'. Demonstrate blending and segmenting the words you make and remind them of how this helps to read new words.

Reading and Discussion

- Ask children to reread the whole story independently, reminding them to look for the patterns and rhymes in the text.
- Explain that while they are reading they should think about how Mo is feeling and whether this makes her behave the way she does.

Returning to the Text for Evaluation and Analysis

- Remind children of the completed first part of Copymaster 1 and reread it together. Ask them if there is anything else important that they have noticed in reading the story again which they would like to change or add.
- Remind children of the task you gave them to think about over the last few days. Ask them to look at the second part of Copymaster 1 and decide whether they think Mo was naughty or not. Remind them that whatever they decide, they must be able to explain why.
- Ask children to tick the 'yes' or 'no' box on their own copy of Copymaster 1 and then write or draw the reason why. When they have finished they should explain their answers to their partners.
- Discuss the different decisions and evaluate the quality of the reasons everyone has given.

Suggested Independent Activities

- Make up the word wheel from Copymaster 2, list all the possible words and check their meanings in a dictionary.
- Using blank word wheels, i.e. the reverse side of the wheel from Copymaster 2, choose a different pattern and fill in the letters. Swap with a partner and find as many words as possible, checking their meanings if necessary.

No! said Mo

Guided Writing (session 1)

Key Objective

- Write about events in personal experience linked to familiar incidents from stories.

Task

Children will write their individual contribution to a group book about their memories of starting school, to help new children as they arrive.

Each child will need Copymaster ❸.
The teacher will need an enlarged copy of Copymaster ❸.

Introduction

- Remind children of the story 'No! said Mo' read in the guided reading session. *How did Mo feel when she got to school?*
- Ask children what they can remember of their first days of school. Help them to access their memories through their senses – can they remember smells they noticed, what their parents said when they left them, the sounds of the school? *How did you feel in the playground and at lunch time? What did you have to eat? Can you remember the taste?* Use role play to help. *You are the teacher now – what did she say? How did she sound? What was her expression like? Can you show us?*

Children Writing Individually

- Using the enlarged Copymaster ❸, model for children writing memories of your own experiences [fictional if necessary], thinking aloud the decisions you are making and emphasising the need to rehearse the writing mentally first.
- Ask children to identify a memory and to write it on Copymaster ❸ in the speech bubble above each figure's head. Encourage them to work out their ideas orally first, and to share them with a partner. Support the paired discussions and, if necessary, scribe the sentences.
- Model the completion of the second part of Copymaster ❸ and then ask children to write their own piece of advice, that will be used to help new children coming to the school next year.

Evaluation

- Collect the completed pages into a group book and share it with some younger children. Ask them if, and in what way, they would have found it helpful when they started school, and invite suggestions for other areas to cover.

Suggested Independent Activity

- Using the advice received from the evaluation, write further pages on the Copymaster ❸ frame, in particular extending the advice section.

No! said Mo

Guided Writing (session 2)

Key Objective

- Use rhymes and patterned stories as models for their own writing.

Task

Children will write an additional page for the story 'No! said Mo', to be added to the book for next year's children.

Each child will need Copymaster 4.

The teacher will need an enlarged copy of Copymaster 4 and some spare copies for extra pages.

Introduction

- Remind children of their previous work on 'No! said Mo' and explain that they are going to make the book even more interesting for the children who read it next by adding some new pages.
- Read together pages 2 to 7 and ask children to identify the words that change [school/music/PE].
- Suggest that to make it more interesting they might also change the name of the teacher and child. Make sure that children can identify the rhyming words and suggest they use their word wheels to find a name to rhyme with 'fun'.

Children Writing Individually

- Using the enlarged version of **Copymaster 4**, read through the prompts with children. Ask them to decide on their own version, alone or in pairs, and to write it on their page. Encourage them to write more pages if they have time.
- Remind children to read their writing through to check that it makes sense.

Evaluation

- Share the new versions with the group and ask everyone to decide whether each new version matches the pattern and has the correct rhymes.

Suggested Independent Activity

- Choose your favourite idea and work on a final version with appropriate illustration, to be inserted into the book.

Is Mo Naughty?

What did she do?

First Mo ______________________________

____

Then Mo ______________________________

____

In the end Mo __________________________

____

Do you think she's naughty?

☐ **Yes**, because ________________________

____

☐ **No**, because _________________________

____

Word Wheel

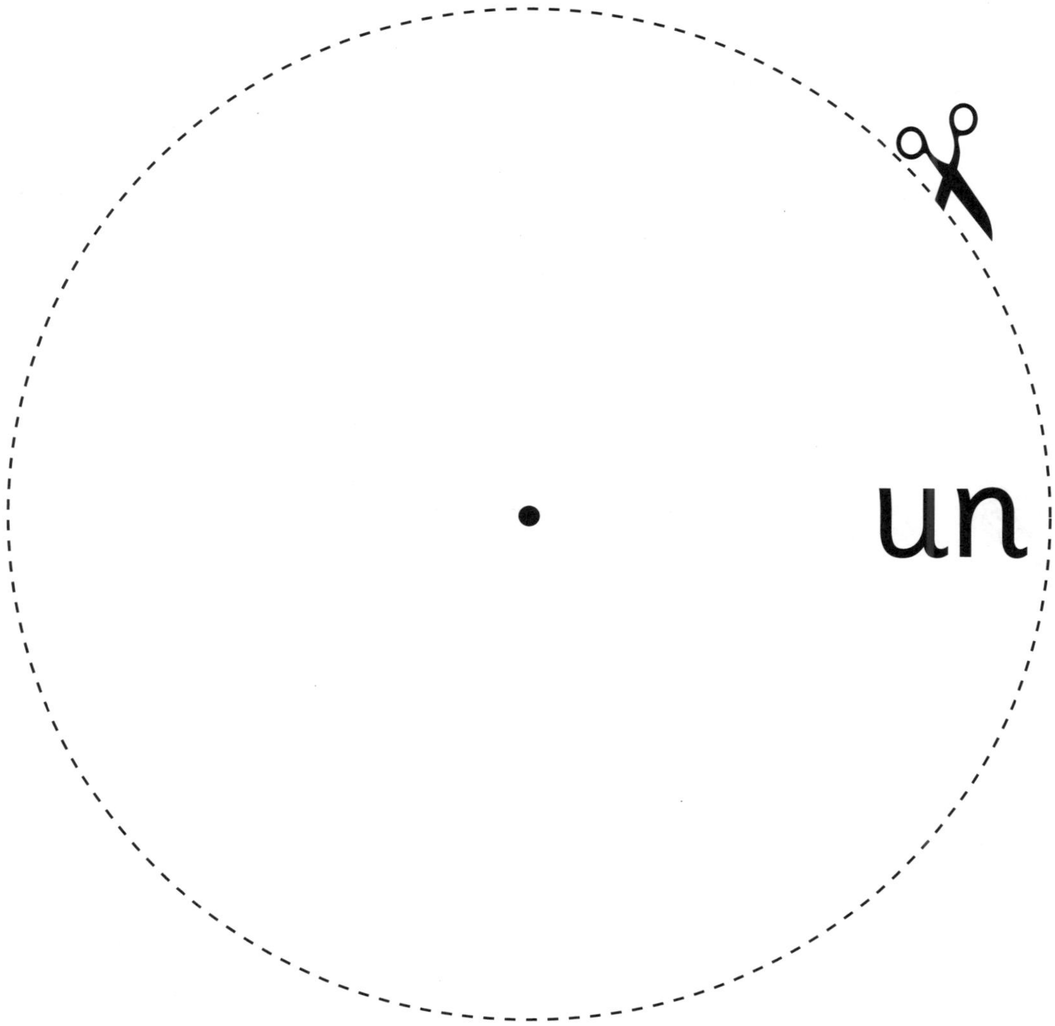

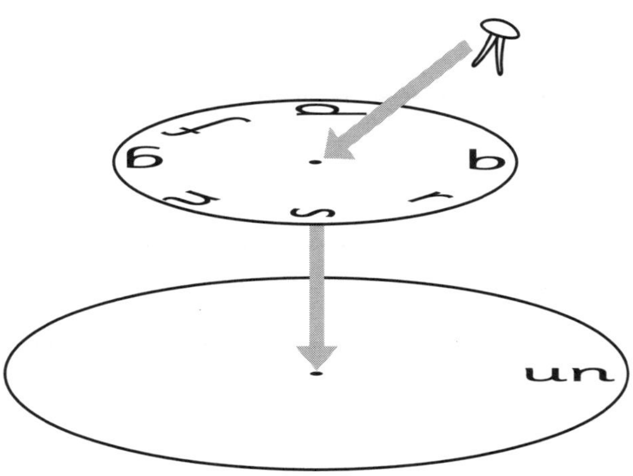

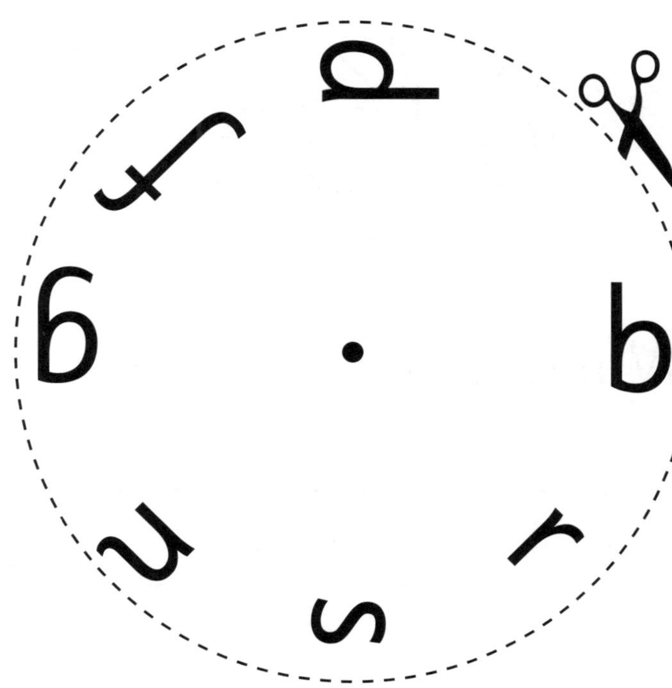

Memories

This is me when I first ______________________

____

I can see ____________

____

____

I can hear ____________

____

____

I can smell ____________

____

____

When you start school ____________________

____

____

____

No!

"Time for ____________________,"

said Miss ______________.

"Time for ____________________.

Time for fun."

"No!" said ______________. "I won't go."

"Time for ____________________,"

said Miss ______________.

"Time for ____________________.

Time for fun."

"No!" said ______________. "I won't go."

Don't Forget!

Guided Reading (session 1)

Key Objectives

- Notice the difference between spoken and written forms through retelling known stories; compare oral versions with the written text.
- Draw on grammatical awareness to read with appropriate expression and intonation.

Introduction

- Ask children to look at the front cover of the book and read the title together. Discuss the meaning of 'naughty'. *What have you ever done that you think is naughty? Is it the same as 'bad' or 'wicked'?*
- Look quickly through the whole book. *What kind of stories do you think these are? What kind of places do they happen in? Are they like fairy stories or more like real life?* [For example, real people rather than talking animals.]
- Explain that we are going to read the story called 'Don't Forget!' and ask the children to find the opening page. *Where is this story happening? Does it look like your kitchen? Who do you think those people are?*
- **Strategy Check**: Recap the range of contextual and phonic strategies the children know. Write the word 'fish' on the whiteboard. Count and say the phonemes and identify together words by analogy [dish, wish].

Reading and Discussion

- Read together pages 12 and 13, discussing any problem words. *What do you notice about the second line on each page?* Model and discuss the effect of the question marks and exclamation marks on the way the words are read. *How could that help you if you were stuck on a word?* [Go back and reread; does the question/answer make sense?]
- Ask children to read pages 14 to 17 independently. *How many fish did the children buy? What size of chips did they buy? Why has the author put 'big' first in italic and then in bold letters?* [To emphasise the importance of the size.]
- Discuss what they think will happen at the end of the story, giving reasons either from the text or from their own experience, and make a note of them to check later. Ask children to read to the end alone.

Returning to the Text for Evaluation and Analysis

- Remind children of their predictions and ask them to discuss with their partner if and how they were accurate. *What has happened to the missing chips? Why has the author put the word 'little' in italics? How do the children feel when they tell Mum they forgot the big bag? How do you know?*
- Divide the roles in the story between children, including a narrator, and reread the full text, pausing to discuss expression and intonation. Notice particularly the difference between the narrator and the characters. Emphasise that the punctuation marks and the style of print are telling us how to read something.

Don't Forget!

Guided Reading (session 2)

Key Objectives

- Notice the difference between spoken and written forms through retelling known stories; compare oral versions with the written text.
- Draw on grammatical awareness to read with appropriate expression and intonation.

Each child will need the character cards cut out from Copymaster 5 and a copy of Copymaster 6.

The teacher will need an enlarged copy of Copymaster 6.

Introduction

- Remind children of the story 'Don't Forget!' read in the last session. *What did the children do that was naughty? What did we find out when we read all the parts aloud?* [We used different expression for different characters and events.] *How did we know what the voices should sound like?* [Punctuation marks.]
- Explain that they are going to retell the story to each other to see if it sounds different from the book, but first they are going to remind themselves of the story.
- **Strategy Check**: Recap the range of contextual and phonic strategies the children know.

Reading and Discussion

- Ask children to read through the whole story independently. Remind them to notice the different voices and emphases in their heads as they read, and of the strategies to use if they get stuck.
- Using **Copymaster 5** model the storytelling process for the children. Choose a character card from the pile and tell the group the story from the character's point of view, showing how you could use the picture as a reminder to 'think yourself' into the role. [The narrator and Mum would make useful examples.]
- Discuss examples of changes that children notice: 'won't' for 'will not'; addition of 'so', 'er', etc.; a change of order in events; a change of emotions.
- Using the enlarged **Copymaster 6**, show children that they have the whole story in front of them and ask them to identify some places where your words were different from the book. Model for them how they might make notes by underlining, circling or highlighting their texts if appropriate.
- Ask children to work with a partner, taking turns to pick up a character card and retelling the story from their viewpoint, while the listener notices some ways this is different from the text.

Returning to the Text for Evaluation and Analysis

- Collect together some of the changes children have noticed between the oral and written versions. Identify the most common and discuss some of the reasons for these, for example: we put in 'er' to give ourselves time to think; add 'So then what do you think happened?' to keep the listener's attention; use hand gestures for size in place of bold type or exclamation marks; use contractions because we speak quickly; use slang or colloquialisms; use different language between children than to an adult, etc.

Don't Forget!

Guided Writing (session 1)

Key Objectives

- Write about events in personal experience linked to familiar incidents from stories.
- Use a capital letter for the personal pronoun 'I' and for the start of a sentence.

Task

Children will write a letter to their mother/sibling/cat/other appropriate 'victim', owning up to, or apologising for, something naughty they did when they were younger.

Each child will need Copymaster 7.
The teacher will need an enlarged copy of Copymaster 7.

Introduction

- Remind children of the story. *What did those children do that was naughty? Do you think Mum realised what they had done or did they get away with it? Do you think she was really angry or just a bit cross? Why?*
- Ask children to think of something that they did when they were younger which they would call naughty, and to share it with their partner. This can be an imaginary event if children can't think of one. [If appropriate, emphasise the previous discussion about the difference between this and something children consider really bad or wicked.]
- Using the enlarged **Copymaster 7**, model the writing of you own 'confession'. Emphasise the help provided by the first section in getting your ideas clear, and talk through the decisions you make: *Who? Oh dear, it was my cat … and my mum. I knocked her favourite vase over by accident. And who got the blame and no treats for a week? … The cat! So now I think I should write to my mum and explain, and ask her to give the cat a big piece of chicken!*
- Make it clear as you write that the writing frame should be changed to fit your particular story, and not allow it to alter what you want to say. As this is a first person narrative, point out as you go the pronoun 'I' and emphasise the need for it to be a capital letter. Show clearly, sentence by sentence, the need for children to form a sentence in their head – and to rehearse it orally – before they write it down. Show also the value of changing your mind, going back, crossing out, rereading, improving.

Children Writing Individually

- Using **Copymaster 7**, ask children to write their own letters, following the strategies you have used. Encourage them to read frequently what they have written so far, both to themselves and a partner, to check for sense and to see if it can be improved.

Evaluation

- Ask children to share the letters they have written and as a group evaluate them in terms of how clear the explanation is of what happened.

Suggested Independent Activities

- Turn the draft letter into a real letter that can be sent by post or hand.
- Share any replies to the letters.

Don't Forget!

Guided Writing (session 2)

Key Objectives

- Write about events in personal experience linked to familiar incidents from stories.
- Re-enact stories in a variety of ways.

Task

To invent, and write a group list of 'useful excuses'.

Each child will need Copymaster 8.

The teacher will need an enlarged copy of Copymaster 8, and a whiteboard and marker pen.

Introduction

- Remind children of the work done before in reading 'Don't Forget!' and in discussing and writing about naughty things that they have done. Review any replies to the letter from the previous session.
- Ask children to look at pages 20 and 21 of the story. *What excuse does Mum suggest for them having so few chips left? Is it a good excuse? Do you think Mum believes it?*
- Ask children to discuss the occasions when they need to think of a good excuse and list them on the whiteboard. Choose one and ask children to act it out in role [e.g. head teacher with pupil apologising for being late], taking a role first yourself if necessary. Explain that the rest of the group are the judges who have to decide whether the excuse is convincing or entertaining enough to be accepted. Encourage children to think creatively and explore the comic possibilities, e.g. 'the dog ate my umbrella'.
- Work through several scenarios, including those on **Copymaster 8**, before choosing one of those to model in written form on the enlarged **Copymaster 8**.

Children Writing Individually

- Ask children to complete the first part of **Copymaster 8**, reminding them to use the good ideas they have tried out orally and to practise their sentences before they write them down.

Evaluation

- Ask children to share their excuses while the group evaluate them for clarity and conviction. Discuss whether the form of the excuse has to change depending on the audience, and if so, how? *Would the same excuse work for your mum and the head teacher? Would you use different words? If your ball hit one of your friends or the head teacher, would you use the same excuse? What would be different?*

Suggested Independent Activity

- Ask children to complete the second part of **Copymaster 8**, using their own scenarios.

Character Cards

Mum

Child 1

Child 2

Narrator

Check the Words!

Mum said,
"Can you go to the chip shop?"
"Yes!" we said.
12

"Can you get three fish and a big bag of chips?"
"Yes!" we said.
13

"Three fish and a *big* bag of chips," said Mum.
"Now don't forget!"
14

"We will not forget!" we said.
15

We went in the chip shop.
We did not forget.
We got three fish and a **big** bag of chips.
16

17

We had one chip.
Then we had two chips.
18

Then we had three chips.
And then we had *lots* of chips!
19

We gave the fish and chips to Mum.
20

"This is a *little* bag of chips," she said.
"Did you forget to get a big bag?"
"Yes," we said.
21

Saying Sorry!

Who I did it to: ______________________________

What I did: ______________________________

Who got the blame: ______________________________

Dear ________________,

Once upon a time, when I was __________

I was __________________________ naughty.

First I ______________________________

Then I ______________________________

In the end I ______________________________

____

I am very sorry ______________________________

Love from ________________

Good Excuses

- I was late for school this morning because

  ____

- I have lost my gloves because ________

  ____

- I have forgotten my PE kit because ______

  ____

- I was __________ because ________

  ____

- I was __________ because ________

  ____

No Tapping!

Guided Reading (session 1)

Key Objectives

- Describe story settings and incidents and relate them to their own experience and that of others.
- Begin using the term 'sentence' to identify sentences in text.

Each child will need Copymaster 9, scissors and glue.
The teacher will need an enlarged copy of Copymaster 9, a whiteboard and marker pen.

Introduction

- Ask children to look at the front cover of the book and read the title together. Discuss the meaning of 'naughty'. *What have you ever done that you think is naughty? Is it the same as 'bad' or 'wicked'?*
- Look quickly through the whole book. *What kind of stories do you think these are? What kind of places do they happen in? Are they like fairy stories or more like real life?* [For example, real people rather than talking animals.]
- Explain that you are going to read the story called 'No Tapping!' and ask the children to find the first page [page 22]. Guide children through the pages, up to page 29, looking quickly at the pictures.
- **Strategy Check**: Recap the range of contextual and phonic strategies the children know. Read pages 22 and 23 together and identify 'tapping'. *Can you see another smaller word inside that one?* Count and say the phonemes for 'tap' and talk about the two meanings.

Reading and Discussion

- Ask children to read independently from the beginning of the story to the end of page 29 and then to predict what will happen next, and why. Note the predictions for checking later. *Why does the first sentence on page 27 have 'No' in italics while the second sentence on page 29 has it in capital letters? What does this tell you about how Dad is feeling?*
- Ask them to read on to the end of the story and to decide whether their prediction was right. *If not, why was it wrong? Was there any evidence you could have found in the text to help you predict correctly?*

Returning to the Text for Evaluation and Analysis

- Praise children for their independent reading and evaluate their predictions and the evidence they used.
- Ask them which of the characters in the story is the one who does something naughty. *What does he do? Does he know that he shouldn't do that? How?* [Dad tells him and the notice says so.] Tell children that there are two reasons why the little brother could be called naughty. Ask them in pairs to work out which naughty things the boy did. [He disobeyed Dad and the notice, and he upset the animals.]
- Explain to children that they are going to think about the order of events in the story. Guide them through the scenes on Copymaster 9. Ask the children to cut out the scenes and place them in the correct order. Remind them to keep rereading the scenes to make sure they make sense in their new order, and to keep checking against the original book. Children can add their own illustrations later.
- Help children to notice key words that also give clues about the order the sentences should be in, e.g. 'then', 'next', 'again'.

No Tapping!

Guided Reading (session 2)

Key Objectives

- Read familiar stories independently.
- Re-enact stories in a variety of ways.

Each child will need Copymaster 10 and their correctly sequenced Copymaster 9.

The teacher will need an enlarged copy of Copymaster 10, and a whiteboard and marker pen.

Introduction

- Remind children of the work done in the previous session. *What does the little brother do in the zoo? What happens because of it? What does it say on the official notice near the frogs? Find the second sentence on page 24 and check. Why has the zoo put that notice up?*
- Explain that today they are going to recount the events of the story themselves, and so first they need to remember exactly what happened.
- **Strategy Check**: Recap the range of contextual and phonic strategies the children know. Identify the word 'frogs' on page 23 and segment it. Discuss and write on the whiteboard any other words they know beginning with 'fr', e.g. 'Friday', 'fry'.

Reading and Discussion

- Ask children to read through the whole story independently.
- Ask them to think, as they are reading, about the order in which the story happens. *Does it matter what order the family saw the animals in? Does it have an effect on the story? What might have happened if they had seen the lion first?*

Returning to the Text for Evaluation and Analysis

- Show children the enlarged copy of **Copymaster 10** and explain that they are going to use this to act out and tell the story. Show clearly the animal enclosures, the pathways and 'viewing points'.
- Begin to retell the story, tracing the route on the paths with a pencil. Demonstrate that there are different routes and solutions, and other animals that the family chose not to visit.
- Ask children to continue with sections of the story as the rest of the group checks that it is in the right order and makes sense.
- Return to the questions about the order of events. *Has anyone now a clearer opinion?*
- Ask children to work with a partner and their own copy of **Copymaster 10** to take turns in drawing the route around the zoo and telling the story to each other.

No Tapping!

Guided Writing (session 1)

Key Objectives

- Write about events in personal experience linked to a variety of familiar incidents from stories.
- Make simple picture storybooks with sentences, modelling them on basic text conventions, e.g. cover, author, title.

Task

Children will plan and write their own story about an event related to familiar experiences and publish it for the class library as an individual book.

Each child will need Copymaster 11.

The teacher will need an enlarged copy of Copymaster 11 and a whiteboard and marker pen.

Introduction

- Remind children about the story they have read in guided reading. *What did the little brother do that was naughty? How did it make Dad feel? How did the older brother feel about it?* Ask children if they have ever done anything naughty like that when they have been told not to.
- Suggest situations where it might have happened – out shopping/playing a game/at meal times/bedtime, etc. Give them time to talk to their partner about this and then share responses, noting them on the whiteboard.
- Using the enlarged Copymaster 11 model planning a story of your own, talking through the decisions you are making. Emphasise that this is a plan, not the finished piece, and so the writing is in note form and not sentences. *Where did this happen? The supermarket. Who? Me and my big sister Margaret and our mum. What? I was carrying my favourite ball and I kept dropping it because it was so big. Mum and Margaret kept shouting at me 'put it in the basket', but I wouldn't. I can't write all that – 'kept on dropping ball' will do. The end? It pushed over a big pile of tins of beans and everyone shouted.*

Children Writing Individually

- Ask children to plan their own stories using their copies of Copymaster 11. Remind them that they are going to use these plans to write a full story and make a book for the library, so they need to be clear.
- Emphasise that these are stories and if children don't have an experience of their own or don't want to use it, they can make one up, use someone else's or adapt yours.

Evaluation

- As a group, review the plans and evaluate them in terms of how useful they will be in writing the final story.
- Discuss other prompts that might help the writing, e.g. a collection of helpful/likely words to have available.

Suggested Independent Activities

- Ask children to read over their plans with a partner and check that their story is complete and makes sense. Ask them to illustrate it to help the reader to understand the story.
- Ask them to list roughly some key words they are likely to use, and think about how they are going to spell them.

No Tapping!

Guided Writing (session 2)

Key Objectives

- Write about events in personal experience linked to a variety of familiar incidents from stories.
- Notice the difference between spoken and written forms.
- Make simple picture storybooks with sentences, modelling them on basic text conventions, e.g. cover, author, title.

Task

Children will plan and write their own story about an event related to familiar experiences and publish it for the class library as an individual book.

Each child will need their own completed copy of Copymaster 11 and an enlarged copy of Copymaster 12 folded as a book.

The teacher will need an enlarged copy of Copymaster 12 folded as a book.

Introduction

- Remind children of the work from the previous session on planning their stories. Explain that the task today is to turn them into complete stories in real books.
- Using the completed **Copymaster 11** for your story, tell the group your story as you intend to write it, i.e. model practising and articulating the story as sentences.
- Invite children to do the same, working with a partner or in the whole group. Encourage them to listen for incomplete phrases that are suitable for an oral, but not written, form.
- Using the enlarged **Copymaster 12**, model the writing of your story. As you work through the book emphasise the layout features and prompts that are incorporated into the sheet – cover/page number/author/illustrator/blurb/price, etc.

Children Writing Individually

- Ask children to work independently to turn their plans into completed books, following your model and leaving until last the covers and the illustrations.
- Support the individual writers, and if necessary scribe the text from dictation.

Evaluation

- Share the completed books and discuss whether they tell interesting stories similar to 'No Tapping!' and if they have made attractive books for others to read in the library. Emphasise the success of having satisfying endings to the stories, and show how this comes from planning the end before beginning the writing.

Suggested Independent Activities

- Complete the front cover with an attractive title. Discuss the kind of lettering that might be used, as well as punctuation marks, referring back to the original book.
- Write a persuasive reason for someone to choose to read this book, and add it to the back cover.
- Complete the illustrations.

All Mixed Up

We looked at the fish next.

He did not tap on the glass again!

Then we had a look at the lions.

We looked at the frogs.

We went to the zoo.

Then we went to see the monkeys.

Let's Visit the Zoo

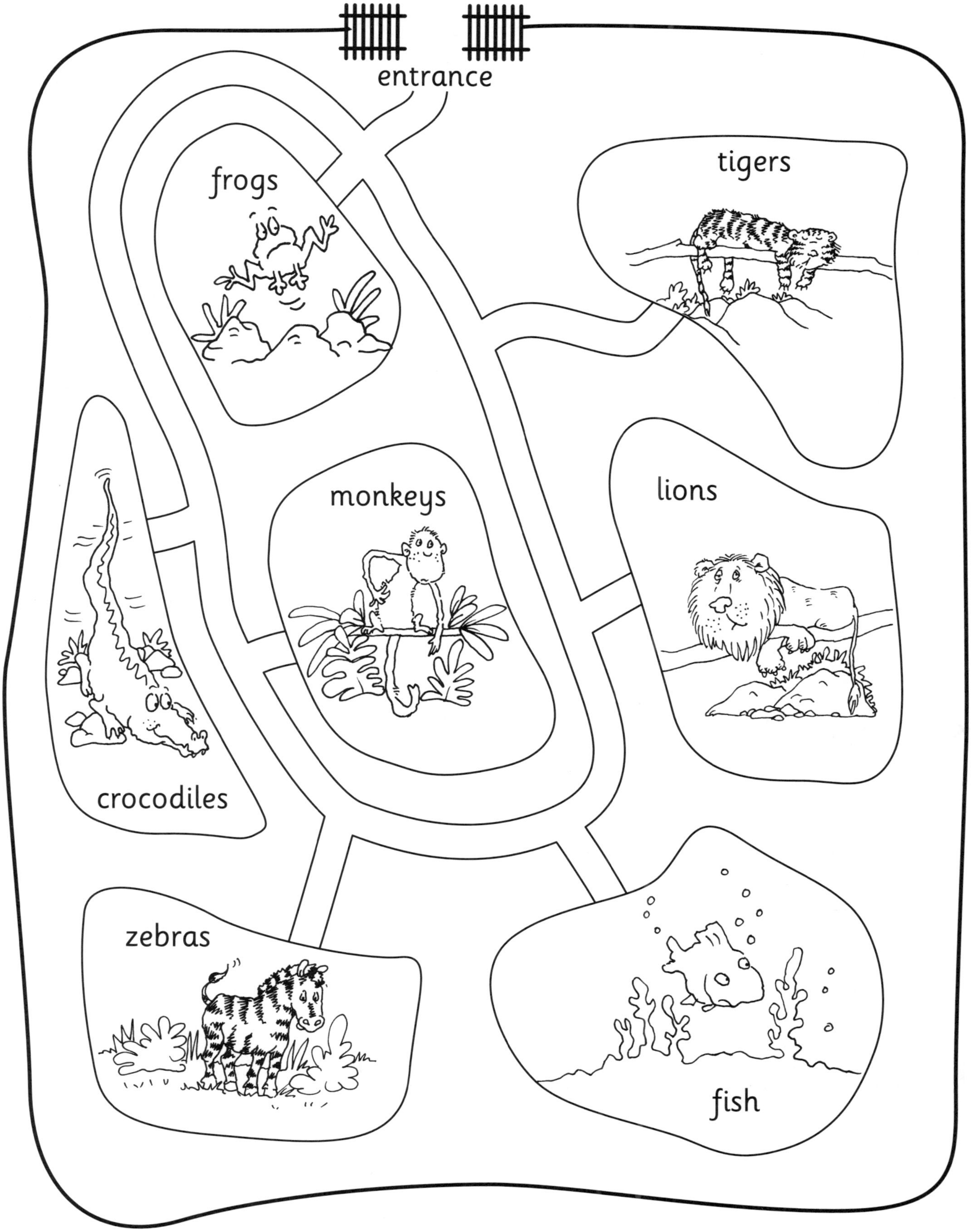

Story Planner

- Where did this happen?

- Who was there?

- What did you/they do?

- What happened in the end?